Pet Care

Written by Vivian Fernandez

Illustration & Design by
Amy McIntyre

Your
Guide
to
Furry
Friends

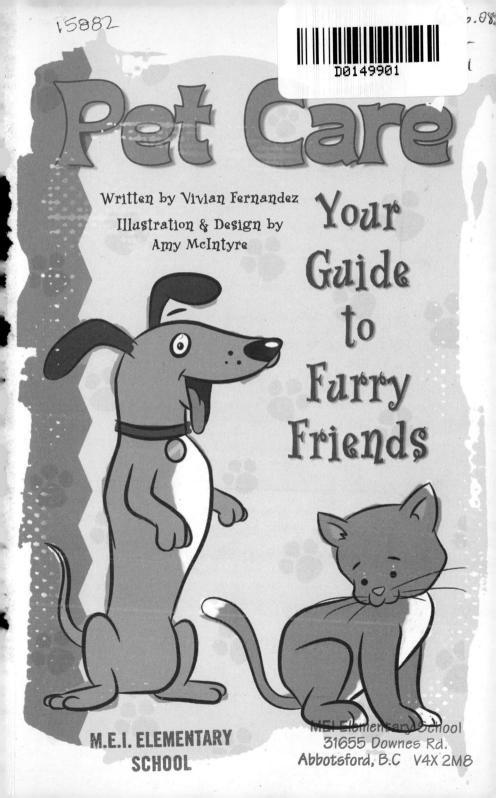

**M.E.I. ELEMENTARY
SCHOOL**

MEI Elementary School
31655 Downes Rd.
Abbotsford, B.C   V4X 2M8

ISBN 1-931623-09-0

Copyright © 2003 by B Plus Marketing, Inc.
All rights reserved.
Published by B Plus Books
765 Silversmith Circle, Lake Mary, FL 32746
Printed in Canada

Written by Vivian Fernandez

Cover Design by Amy McIntyre
Design by Amy McIntyre

Reviewed by Lissette R. Esteban, D.V. M.
Kirkpatrick Veterinary Hospital
Orlando, Florida

Contents

CHAPTER 1:
Which Pet Is Right For Me?

You've wanted a pet for a long time, and now you're ready to get one. But which pet is best for you? Both dogs and cats need care every day. Dogs need a little more care because they're usually bigger, and they depend on you to take them out for walks (and to clean up after them). Dogs and cats can live for more than 10 years-that's a long time for you to promise to care for a pet. It's a big responsibility, but you'll end up with what may be the best friend you'll ever have.

In this book you'll read about some of the most important things you need to know about having a pet. But first there's a quick quiz you can take-just for fun to see which pet might be best for you, especially if you haven't decided if you want a dog, a cat, or maybe just want to start things slow by getting some kind of a digital pet. To take the quiz, read the first sentence under START HERE. Then follow the [art showing solid arrow line] path if the sentence describes you, or the [art showing dotted arrow line] path if it doesn't.

DOG

M.E.I. ELEMENTARY
SCHOOL

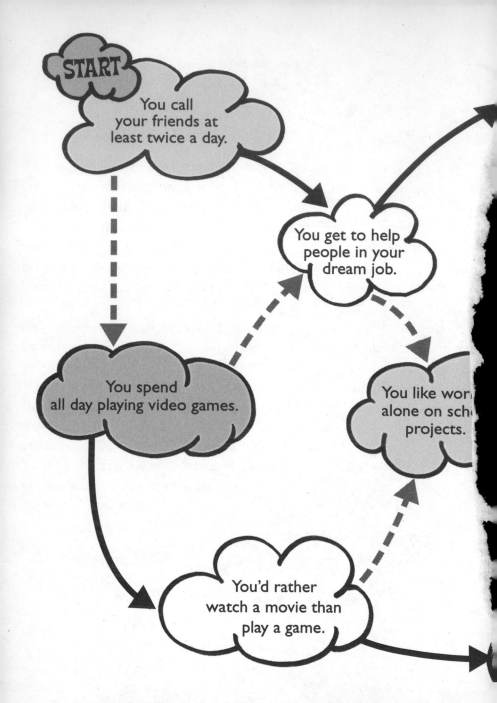

START

You call your friends at least twice a day.

You get to help people in your dream job.

You spend all day playing video games.

You like wor[king] alone on sch[ool] projects.

You'd rather watch a movie than play a game.

Now that you've finished the pet quiz, is a dog, a cat, or a digital pet the best choice for you? If your path led you to a dog or a cat, turn to page 13 to read more about your choice. If your path led you to a digital pet, turn to page 59 to learn more about these special kinds of pets.

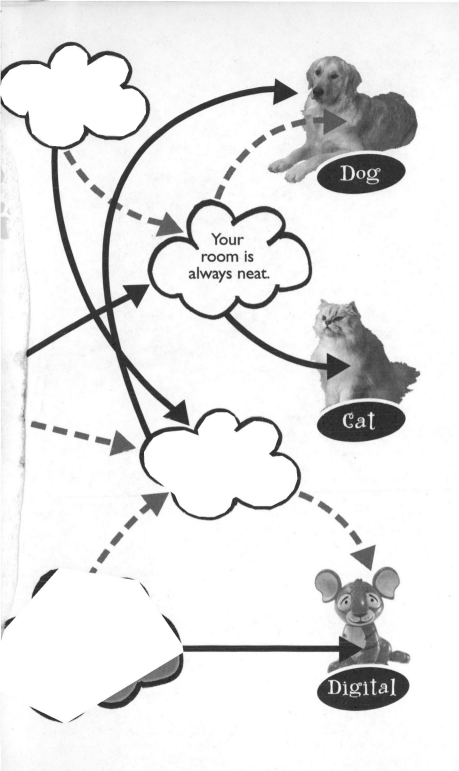

Your room is always neat.

Dog

Cat

Digital

CHAPTER 2:
Questions, Questions

You've made one decision—you want a dog or a cat. But there are still plenty of questions to ask. First of all, does the place where you live allow any pets? Make sure you know the answer to this before you get excited about bringing home a new pet. Then ask yourself the following questions so you have a plan when you go get your pet.

What Kind?

There are many different breeds, or kinds, of dogs and cats. A purebred dog or cat means that both of its parents belong to the same breed. A mixed-breed dog or cat means that its parents belonged to different breeds.

Different breeds of dogs and cats have different personalities. And certain breeds of dogs and cats need more attention than others—they may have longer coats, or they may like to play more. To find out about different dog or cat breeds, ask your friends with pets, check out books from the library, or look on the Internet.

What Size?

The size of the pet you get depends on the size of your home, and if you have a large backyard or a park nearby where you can take your pet for exercise. Adult cats don't get too big, so any size home is okay for them. But dogs can weigh anywhere from less than 7kg (15.4lb) to more than 45kg (99lb). Having a large dog cooped up inside a small apartment all day isn't very fair to the dog. You need to know the size of the adult dog; a small puppy can grow to be a very big dog when he's an adult. Also, you need to know if there are any rules for what size pet you can have where you live. Some apartment buildings don't allow dogs that are heavier than a certain weight.

What Age?

Puppies and kittens can be a lot of fun, but they are also a lot of extra work. Their playfulness can get them into quite a bit of trouble, and you'll also spend more time training them. If you get an older dog or cat, it's probably already trained. But it may also have some bad habits that will be harder for you to change. And the older the dog or cat is, there more health problems it may have.

What Laws?

No matter where you live, there are pet-related laws you need to know about. It's important that you know what these laws are before you get your new dog or cat. The laws cover things like your pet's health, making sure people around your pet are kept safe, and your responsibilities if your pet hurts someone. For example, you probably need a license for your new dog or cat. You also need to make sure your pet has its rabies vaccination. And if you have a dog, there might be laws about keeping it on a leash, cleaning up after it in public, and making sure your dog's barking doesn't keep your neighbors up at night. You can find pet laws at your library, municipal hall, Humane Society, or check with your veterinarian.

What About Health?

Have the name of a veterinarian before you bring home your new dog or cat. Ask friends and family members with pets for the names of their veterinarians. Then you'll have a list of doctors you can trust from which you can choose your veterinarian.

Where Should You Get Your Pet?

There are several places you can go to get a new dog or cat. If you want a purebred, your best chance is a professional or private breeder. Just understand that buying a dog or a cat from a breeder can cost several hundred dollars. But people can give you a lot of information about the animal, such as its health and its personality.

Animal shelters are less expensive places to find a pet. You'll probably see mostly mixed-breeds, but you'll find dogs and cats of all ages and sizes. Getting an animal from a shelter may mean that you won't get a lot of information about its history. But the GREAT thing is that you'll be giving a home to an animal that needs it!

You can also check with veterinarians in your area. Sometimes they know people with pets that just had puppies or kittens. Or try asking your friends.

Wherever you go to get your new pet, look for these signs to make sure that it's healthy.

Dogs

- Eyes are clear
- Ears aren't swollen or sensitive when you touch them
- Ears don't have a bad smell
- Coat has no bare spots
- Gums are pink and healthy
- Skin has no bumps, scabs, or red patches
- Dog is alert, energetic, and responds to you

Cats

- Eyes are clear
- Ears aren't swollen, itchy, or sensitive when you touch them
- Coat has no bare spots
- Gums are pink and healthy
- Mouth doesn't have a bad smell
- Skin has no lumps, swellings, or scabs
- Whiskers are long and not broken
- Paw pads have no cracks
- Cat is curious, energetic, and responds to you

Chapter 3:
Your New Dog

Dogs need more attention and training than other pets. But for your hard work, you get a companion that always wants to make you happy and is by your side when you need a friend or a protector. That's why dogs have the nickname of "man's best friend." And they've been our best friends for more than 10,000 years—longer than any other pet.

There are more than 300 breeds of dogs. Long ago people depended on dogs to help them hunt or work. Sometimes people still use dogs for these reasons. But now most people choose a dog because they like how it looks. Kennel clubs usually put all breeds of dogs into one of seven groups, depending on what that breed of dog was meant to do.

Sporting dogs were meant to help hunters that use guns. These dogs pointed their bodies toward hidden game (the animal that is being hunted). Some dogs in this group are pointers, retrievers, and spaniels.

Hounds were developed to hunt. They caught and killed the game themselves, or they caught and held the game until the hunter came to kill it. Some dogs in this group are beagles, greyhounds, and dachshunds.

Working dogs worked by guarding or pulling sleds. Some dogs in this group are Siberian huskies, boxers, and Rottweilers. **Terriers** were meant to dig and hunt small game, such as rabbits. Some dogs in this group are Scottish terriers, Jack Russell terriers, and Miniature Schnauzers.

Toy dogs were bred to be pets. Some dogs in this group are chihuahuas, Pugs, and toy poodles.

Non-sporting dogs are large companion dogs that were once meant to work or hunt. Some dogs in this group are bulldogs, chow chows, and Dalmations.

Herding dogs looked after sheep and cattle so the animals couldn't get away from the group. Some dogs in this group are collies, German shepherds, and Pulik.

No matter which breed you choose, or if you choose a mixed-breed dog, your new friend is going to fill your days with lots of play, excitement, and love!

Dog Facts

• Dogs come in many different sizes. The smallest breed is the chihuahua. The heaviest are the mastiffs and St. Bernards. The tallest are the Irish wolfhounds and the Great Danes.

• Dogs have a great sense of smell and can smell things people can't. Bloodhounds can even pick up a scent trail that is four days old.

• Dogs can hear better than people, and can hear sounds people can't.

• Dogs see differently than people. Dogs see most colors in shades of gray, and they can't tell the difference between the colors green, red, yellow, and orange. But dogs can see movement much better than people.

• Dogs have a special group of cells in the backs of their eyes. The tapetum lucidum reflects light inside a dog's eye to help it see in low light. The tapetum lucidum is also what makes a dog's eyes glow when a light shines on its eyes in the dark.

• Dogs don't have sweat glands like we do, so they pant to help stay cool.

What Do I Need?

To make your dog more comfortable in his new home, you should have everything ready for him. From food, to a collar, to a bed just for him, have all of the supplies you need before you pick him up. (Look on page 62 for a list of things you'll need that you can copy and take with you when you shop.) On the next few pages you'll find the most important supplies you'll need for your new dog, and learn why you need them.

Food and Water

Whether it's a quick snack or a complete dinner, you have lots of food choices. The same is true for dogs. Besides canned food, semi-moist food, and dry food, there's also food made just for puppies, dogs with allergies, and more. The best (and easiest) way to choose what food to feed your dog is to ask an expert, such as your veterinarian.

Your dog will need a bowl for his food and a separate bowl for his water. Mealtimes can be exciting times for dogs, so buy bowls that have a rubber bottom or are heavy enough so they don't get pushed around the floor. Bowls made of metal, ceramic, stainless steel, or glass are better choices than plastic bowls. Plastic bowls may get scratches where bacteria can grow and make your dog sick. Some dogs may develop a rash on their chins if they eat out of plastic bowls. Set up the food and water bowls in a spot that your dog can easily get to, but not in the way so people trip over them. A plastic mat under the bowls will help keep the area clean and dry.

Most dogs older than one year need to be feed twice a day. Puppies need to be feed more often, depending on their age and weight. Check with your veterinarian to be sure about how often to feed your dog.

As soon as you bring your new dog home, get into the habit of feeding him at the same time every day. This gives him a routine so he knows when it's feeding time. Choose a feeding time when you have plenty of time after to take him for a walk so he can relieve himself. Any uneaten moist or semi-moist food that's been sitting out for more than half an hour should be thrown away. His food bowl should always be clean between feedings. Dogs need a lot of fresh water, so change his water at least twice a day, making sure his water bowl is always filled. Clean both the food and water bowls with soap and water a couple of times a week (don't use any bleaches or strong chemicals).

Although many people give dogs scraps from their plate, it's safer not to. Some foods may make your dog sick. Also, feeding your dog people food may make him gain too much weight.

These are just SOME of the foods that can be especially dangerous for your dog:
- chocolate
- moldy foods
- small bones, such as chicken bones
- raw meat

If you decide to feed your dog a different kind of dog food, do it slowly. Changing his food from one day to the next may give him an upset stomach, or he may simply refuse to eat. Mix in a little of the new food with the old food. After a couple of days mix in more of the new food so you have a mixture that is half old food and half new food. After a couple of days fill your dog's bowl with mostly new food and a little of the old food. A couple of days after that, your dog should be ready for a bowl with just the new food.

Crate

A crate can be used as a place for your dog to sleep, it can help when you housetrain him, and it can be used for traveling. (For steps to train your dog, see page 27.) Crates are made of molded plastic or open wire. The crate needs to be big enough for your dog to stand up, lie down, and turn in a circle. Add a few dog toys and a water bowl if he's going to be inside the crate for more than an hour.

It may seem cruel, but getting your dog used to being confined to his crate is very important. If you let your dog roam freely in your home when no one is there, he's sure to get into trouble by relieving himself where he shouldn't, chewing up your right sneaker, or knocking over your mom's favorite lamp. With a puppy, you shouldn't leave him in a crate more than one hour equal to his age in months. So, if your puppy is two months old he can stay in the crate for two hours at a time; if he's five months old, five hours. A seven-hour stretch is the longest any dog should be left in a crate.

Before you confine your dog to his crate, take him outdoors to give him a chance relieve himself and to get some exercise. He shouldn't be confined to a small space if he hasn't first had a chance to use up some energy. Start training him to follow commands by saying, "Crate!" and throwing a food treat inside the crate. Eventually, stop using the treat.

Dog Bed

Your dog should have a bed he can call his own. Letting your new dog sleep in your bed isn't a good idea. If he's not housetrained he may have accidents in your bed. And the small puppy that only takes up a small spot on your bed by your feet may take up a lot more of your bed when he's an adult. You can buy a bed or use his crate or a box with soft blankets inside. Wicker baskets aren't good for puppies that are still at their chewing stage. Your dog's bed should be big enough that he can stretch out in it. If you have a puppy, get a bed big enough to fit him when he's an adult.

For the first week or so, put his bed in a room that's not too big and can be cleaned up easily, such as the bathroom. (Just be sure all cleaners and other dangers are in cupboards he can't get into.) Keeping him in a small area will help him feel less stressed. It will also keep him from getting into trouble while everyone's asleep.

Grooming Tools

Whether you have a dog with short hair or one with long hair, you'll need a brush. Most dogs love being brushed and it gives both of you more time to spend together. There are different kinds of brushes and combs for the different kinds of coats dogs have. Make sure the comb and brush you buy is right for your dog. Longhaired dogs also need more brushing than shorthaired dogs.

Brush your **long-haired dog** once a day. Start by gently brushing his back, stomach, legs, neck and finally head. Brush in the direction that his hair grows. If you find a knot, use your fingers to untangle it. Be careful not to pull too hard on his hair. Then use a wide-toothed comb all over his body.

Dogs with **short-haired coats** only need to be brushed once or twice a week. Like with long-haired coats, gently brush your dog all over his entire body.

You'll also need a fine-toothed comb to check for fleas. The best places to look for fleas are on your dog's stomach or other areas where he has less hair. Fleas look like dark sesame seeds (and they'll jump or move very quickly) and their droppings look like black pepper. If you see either, it's time for a flea bath. You or a professional groomer can bathe your dog. If you choose to do it, bathe him in lukewarm water with flea shampoo made especially for dogs. Make sure you buy the right shampoo for his age and follow the instructions on the label carefully.

Next check his bed for fleas. If you see any, you'll need to wash his bed in hot water. If his bed isn't washable, you may need to buy a new one. If the fleas are all over your home, you'll need to take care of that by calling an exterminator. Make sure you check with your veterinarian to find out if your dog needs any special medication to treat him for fleas.

Most dogs don't need frequent baths. Brushing and combing gets rid of most of it and too much bathing can be bad for his skin and coat. But since there are times he will need one, it's a good idea to bathe him once a month so he knows what to expect when it's bath time. And if you live somewhere with warm weather, you may need to bathe him every two weeks.

Before you start his bath, give him a good brushing. Make sure his coat is free of all tangles and mats (mats not taken care of before shampooing may trap soap). If your dog has a lot of mats, it might be best to take him to a groomer.

Have everything ready before you start the bath. Depending on his size, you can use the bathtub or bathroom sink. ***Beware: you WILL get wet!*** And if he decides to shake himself while he's wet, your bathroom will probably need some drying off, too. So if the weather is warm and sunny you might want to bathe him outdoors in a plastic or metal tub. You'll also need dog shampoo, a large cup (for pouring water) or a hose, and a towel.

Wet your dog with lukewarm water. Then squeeze some shampoo onto his back and massage it into his coat. Start at his neck. If your dog has long hair gently squeeze the shampoo into his coat instead of massaging it or you may tangle his coat. Rinse him off with water, starting at the head and moving down to his tail. Make sure he has no soap left in his coat. You may need to rinse him several times.

Take him out of the tub and wrap him in the towel. Gently press the towel to his fur to squeeze out the water. Don't rub the towel or he will end up with tangles. You can try using a hair dryer, but the noise may scare him. If you decide to use the hair dryer keep the heat on low so he isn't burned. You can also just let him air dry in the sun or in a warm spot indoors.

Another grooming tool you'll need is a dog nail clipper. If done correctly clipping your dog's nails isn't painful. However, that doesn't mean he will like it. If you clip his nails once a week, he will get used to it quicker.

You may to have want your veterinarian show you how to clip you dog's nails before you try it on your own. At home, you may want to have an adult helper until you and your dog are comfortable with the procedure. Choose a time when your dog is calm. Speaking calmly to him and telling him what a good boy he's being while you're trimming will help keep him calm.

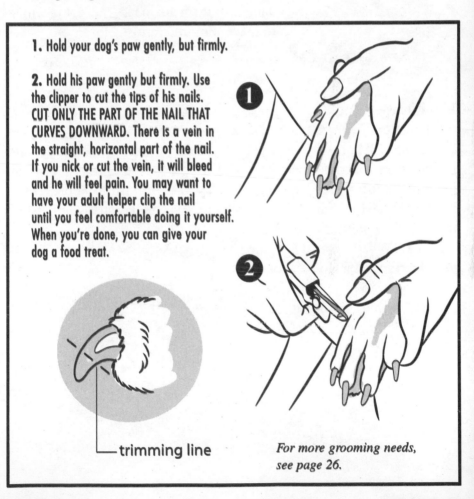

1. Hold your dog's paw gently, but firmly.

2. Hold his paw gently but firmly. Use the clipper to cut the tips of his nails. CUT ONLY THE PART OF THE NAIL THAT CURVES DOWNWARD. There is a vein in the straight, horizontal part of the nail. If you nick or cut the vein, it will bleed and he will feel pain. You may want to have your adult helper clip the nail until you feel comfortable doing it yourself. When you're done, you can give your dog a food treat.

trimming line

For more grooming needs, see page 26.

Leash

A leash is a must for taking your dog on walks and for training him. Choose a leash that's right for your dog's size. Be sure the clip is sturdy enough to stay attached to the collar.

Collar

You'll use the collar to hold on to your dog with your hand or a leash, so it needs to be well made. There are different kinds of collars. For everyday use, you should probably buy a buckle collar. The collar should be tight enough on him so that he can't slip it off his head, but not too tight to make him uncomfortable.

Identification Tag

No matter how well you watch over your dog, there's always a chance he will get away from you. If you don't want to spend days and nights worried about where he is and if you'll ever find him, have an identification tag ready for him the day you bring him home. Don't have a name for him yet? No problem. Just make sure *your* name, telephone number, and address are on the tag. When you visit the veterinarian, find out about having your dog tattooed or injected with a microchip for a more permanent kind of identification.

Toys

Your dog will love having a few toys to play with—and it'll keep him happy when you're not around. Toys should be made especially for dogs; you don't want your very playful dog tearing his new toy to pieces in the first few minutes. Also, the toys should be large enough so he can't swallow them. If you have a puppy, be sure to get him nylon or other toys made for chewing so he doesn't chew on your shoes instead!

Take time every day to get your dog to run around and play. Find a place outdoors where you can throw him a ball and play fetch. Or just chase him around, and then let him chase you. Playtime for your dog is also a way for him to exercise his mind and his body.

Dog-Proofing Your Home

Dogs are pretty good at staying out of trouble, but they do need some help from you. Careless behavior from you might make your home a dangerous place for your new friend. So a day before he joins you, give your home a safety inspection.

Put away anything small that can be swallowed. Keep electrical cords tucked away so he won't be tempted to chew them. Anything breakable that's on a table that he might bump into—or knock over with his happily wagging tail—should be put somewhere safer. Shoes left lying around are too tempting for him NOT to chew if he's teething.

Some things can make your dog sick or even poison him. Make sure all pesticides (including roach and ant traps) and household cleaners are kept behind closed cabinet or closet doors. Keep all medicines where he can't reach them. Some plants are also dangerous to dogs. This list shows some of the more common plants that should be kept out of homes with dogs. If you're not sure about a plant, check with your veterinarian to make sure it's safe for your dog.

Car Travel Safety

Dangerous Plants

Azalea	Fox glove	Oleander
Cactus	Iris	Poinsettia
Delphinium	Larkspur	Rhododendron
Dumb cane	Laurel	Wisteria
English ivy	Mistletoe	

Car Travel Safety

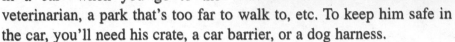

There are times when you
need to take your dog with you
in a car—when you go to the
veterinarian, a park that's too far to walk to, etc. To keep him safe in
the car, you'll need his crate, a car barrier, or a dog harness.

If your dog's crate is the metal-wire kind and it fits in the car, use
that. He's already comfortable using it, and the wire crate lets plenty of
air move around him.

A car barrier can be a plastic net or a metal or plastic screen that keeps
your dog in a separate part of the car (such as the back seat or the back
section of a mini-van). Your dog can still move around, but he can't
jump into the front seat where he may be hurt if there's an accident.

The dog harness is like a seat belt for dogs. It hooks up to the seat
belts in your car and lets your dog move around a little, but keeps him
safe in case of an accident. However, these harnesses can be expensive
and some dogs may not like using them.

Make sure your dog has plenty of air when he's in the car. You can
have the air conditioner on or open some windows. If you do open
windows, make sure you have screens for the windows to keep your
dog safe. These screens are usually made of plastic and can be taken
off the windows when your dog isn't in the car.

DON'Ts for Car Travel

DON'T let your dog ride on the drivers lap. It's not safe for the dog or the driver.
DON'T let your dog stick his head out of the window when the car is moving. Flying bits
of dirt can injure his eyes.
DON'T leave your dog in a parked car. It can get VERY hot in a car, even if it's parked
in the shade and the windows are left open a few inches. Heatstroke can happen in just
a few minutes, and your dog can die.

The Well-Groomed Dog

Besides brushing and bathing, your dog needs a little help to look his best. That means you need to keep his eyes, ears, and teeth clean. Imagine what your teeth would look like if you never brushed them! And besides looking great, a well-groomed dog is a healthier dog.

Eyes

Check his eyes every day for any discharge. Use a tissue or a wet cotton ball to gently wipe around his eyes. If you notice that his eyes are puffy, red, or have a lot of discharge, you should call your veterinarian. (For more signs that you may need to call the veterinarian, see page 37.)

Ears

After you check your dog's eyes, check his ears. Look for dirt, waxy buildup, and grainy, dry discharge (this could mean he has ear mites). Put a drop of ear-cleaning solution (made for dogs) on a cotton ball and wipe the inside of his ear flaps. Then put a drop of the solution on a cotton swab and clean his ear canals. Because you need to be very careful not to go too deep into his canals, you may want to ask your veterinarian to show you how to do it the first time. If you notice that the inside of his ears are red, there is a bad smell, or you find ear mites, you should call your veterinarian. (For more signs that you may need to call the veterinarian, see page 37.)

Teeth

Finally, brush your dog's teeth. Just like with your teeth, if your dog has bad tooth decay he will need the tooth pulled. You can wrap a small piece of cloth around your finger and rub your finger across your dog's teeth. Pay extra attention to the teeth next to his cheeks. You can also use a small toothbrush and toothpaste made especially for dogs. If you notice that his gums are pale or swollen and his breath smells especially bad, you should call your veterinarian. (For more signs that you may need to call the veterinarian, see page 37.)

Paper Training or Housetraining?

There are two ways to train your dog to relieve himself— paper train or housetrain. Paper training means your dog is trained to relieve himself on newspaper in a spot you have chosen. With paper training there will always be some smell and some mess in your home, and it's probably not a good idea for larger dogs. Housetraining means your dog can "hold it" until you take him outdoors. Housetraining can

take more time and you must be able to take your dog outdoors on a schedule so he can relieve himself. Whichever way you choose, it will take at least three weeks for your dog to be fully trained.

Your dog needs to be at least nine weeks old before you can start trying to train him. (He may not have the muscle control he needs if he is younger.) And he can only hold it for about one hour for every month of age. So don't expect your five-month-old puppy to wait more than five hours to relieve himself.

Paper Training

Decide where you want your dog to relieve himself. It should be a small, confined area. His crate or a bathroom is a good place. You'll need to keep him in this area until he's trained. But make sure you let him out for plenty of playtime with you, and don't keep him in the crate longer than he should be. (Remember, that's one hour for each month of age.) Once you choose a spot, stick with it. If you change spots he will be confused and the training will take longer.

- Cover a small area of his crate or the bathroom floor with three layers of newspaper.
- Whenever your dog finishes eating, drinking, playing, sleeping, or looks like he has to go (he walks in a circle or sniffs the floor), give him a command, such as "Bathroom!" and put him down on the newspaper. You may need to keep a hand on him so he doesn't walk away. (But don't pet him.) Make sure he stays on the newspaper until he relieves himself. When he does, praise him.
- Remove the top two layers of newspaper after he finishes. Put down more newspaper under the leftover layer. He will be able to smell the scent of what he did there (even though you probably won't) and it'll remind him of what he's supposed to do there.
- When your dog starts relieving himself right after you put him on the newspaper, he's ready to start walking over there by himself. Walk over to the paper, give him the command, and wait for him to come and relieve himself. Eventually, he will go without needing your commands.

- When your dog has gone a week without making a mistake, you can start letting him into other rooms of your home or out of his crate more often. Just be sure to keep a close eye on him so you can correct him if he has an accident.

> If you catch your dog relieving himself where he's not supposed to, say "No!" and put him on the newspaper. When he finishes on the paper, praise him.
>
> If you don't catch him in the act, don't yell at him. He won't remember what he did wrong so he won't know why you're yelling at him. If you find a spot where he had an accident, clean and deodorize the area or he may smell it and keep relieving himself there.

Housetraining

It takes more time to housetrain a dog, but it's worth it. There's less smell and mess in your home, and you can take your dog with you anywhere you go because he can relieve himself anywhere outdoors. Like with paper training, you'll need to keep him confined to a small area, such as the bathroom or his crate, until he's trained. Make sure you let him out for plenty of playtime and don't keep him in the crate longer than he should be. (One hour for each month of age.)

Decide on a place—your backyard, a nearby park-that you can always walk to with your dog until he's trained. Always take the same route so he gets used to the routine. Make sure you know about any pooper-scooper laws. Most places require that your dog is on a leash and that you pick up any mess he makes.

- Whenever your dog finishes eating, drinking, playing, sleeping, or looks like he has to go (he walks in a circle or sniffs the floor), give him a command, such as "Out!" and put him on the leash. Then walk him to the place you chose.
- When you get to the spot, walk back and forth with him on the leash until he starts to relieve himself. Then give him a command, such as "Bathroom!" so he knows what the command means. When he's done, praise him.

- When your dog has gone a week without making any mistakes indoors, you can start letting him into other rooms of your home or out of his crate more often. Just be sure to keep a close eye on him so you can correct him if he has an accident. (To correct your dog when he has an accident, see page 29.)

Training Your Dog

The best way to train your dog is to go to an obedience-training program with certified instructors. These people are experts in how dogs learn and they have lots of practice training dogs. You can ask your veterinarian or friends and family members for trainers and programs they recommend.

However, you may have to wait some time before you can get your dog into the class you want. Most places don't train dogs younger than eight weeks old. Or maybe the program you chose is in the middle of its session and won't start a new one for another two weeks. That doesn't mean you should let your dog run around doing whatever he wants. If you do, training will be tougher for both of you. So here are some tips for training your dog in the basics before you get to class. Start with heel, then sit, then stay, then down, then come. This order is important because he needs to know one command to move on to the next command.

DO's and DON'Ts for Training

- DO have a handful of dog food treats close by for rewards.

- DO make sure your dog is wearing his leash and collar.

- DON'T try to train your dog when he's tired, needs to relieve himself, or just ate.

- DON'T train for longer than five minutes at a time.

- DO make your command, praise, and correction voices sound different.
  Say commands such as "Sit!" or "Stay!" clearly and firmly.
  Give praise such as "Good boy!" using a happy voice.
  Correct by saying "No!" sharply, but without yelling.

- DON'T EVER hit your dog. You can hit the ground in front of him with your hand to stress a correction, but NEVER hit him.

- DO let him know when the training session is complete by releasing him with an "Okay!" command and unleashing him.

Heel

1. While your dog is standing or sitting, hold his leash and stand a few steps away with him on your left side.

2. Say his name and give the command "Heel!" while GENTLY giving the leash a quick tug, then start walking. Praise him as he walks by your side. Practice the heel command for a couple of minutes before releasing him with an "Okay!" command.

3. As you keep training, make things more complicated by walking in circles and zig-zag patterns. You want him to heel at your side no matter where or how you walk. Always praise him for keeping up with you.

4. If he stops heeling (he starts walking away from you or just refuses to walk), correct him. GENTLY give the leash a quick tug and say "No!" Then start over.

Sit

1. While your dog is standing, hold his leash and stand so he's on your left side.

Show your dog a food treat and hold it over his head.

2. Say "Sit!" and move the treat back over his head to his rear. As he follows the treat, his body will probably lower into a sit position. If he doesn't automatically sit, give the command again and with one hand use the leash to gently hold his head up and with your other hand press gently behind his back legs to lower him into a sitting position.

3. When he's sitting, give him the treat and praise him.

4. If he doesn't sit, don't correct him. He hasn't learned what to do yet, so he's not actually doing anything wrong. Walk away, wait a few moments, then try again.

5. Practice the sit command until your training time is over.

Stay

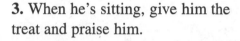

1. While your dog is sitting, hold his leash and stand so he's on your left side.

2. Say "Stay!" and hold the palm of your hand that isn't holding the leash in front of his nose.

3. If he stays sitting, praise him, say "Okay!" and let him walk away.

4. If he does not stay sitting, correct him. GENTLY give the leash a quick tug and say "No!" Then have him sit and start over.

5. Each time you train him to stay, walk a little further away and have him stay a few seconds longer before releasing him. (You'll probably need to give him the command more than once as you have him stay for longer amounts of time.) Start by holding your palm in front of his nose; then walking in front of him; then taking steps, one at a time, away from him. Praise him every time he stays sitting, and then release him with an "Okay!" command. Whenever he doesn't stay, correct him and try again. Don't practice the stay command more than two or three times in one session.

6. Keep practicing the stay command until your dog can stay for three minutes after only one command.

Down

1. While your dog is sitting, hold his leash and kneel so he's on your left side. In your other hand, hold a food treat.

2. Hold the food treat in front of his nose. Say "Down!" and lower the food treat so he starts to lower himself. Then move the treat a little away from him. You can gently tug down on the leash as you lower the treat.

3. When he is down, praise him and let him have the treat.

4. If he gets up instead of going down, correct him. GENTLY give the leash a quick tug and say "No!" Then have him sit and start over.

5. Add the stay command so he stays down until you release him. Practice the down command until he can stay down for at least 15 minutes before you release him with an "Okay!" command. To do this, follow the steps you did when teaching him to stay by taking steps further and further away over several training sessions.

Come

1. While your dog is sitting, hold his leash and stand so he's on your left side.

2. Say "Stay!" and take two steps away from him.

3. Say his name and then the command "Come!"

4. As soon as he starts moving toward you, praise him.

5. If he doesn't come to you, correct him. GENTLY give the leash a quick tug and say "No!" Then start over.

6. Each time you train him to come, walk a little further away. Keep practicing until your dog comes to you when you're several feet away.

What's My Dog Trying To Tell Me?

To figure out what your dog is trying to tell you, you have to learn his language. Your dog "talks" to you with sounds, such as barks, and with his body, like when he wags his tail. As you get to know your dog, you'll know by how he behaves if he's happy, scared, or wants to be left alone.

When your dog is happy and relaxed he might...
- roll over and show you his belly.
- quickly wag his tail back and forth.

When your dog wants to play he might...
- stand with his back legs straight up, bend down on his front legs, and wag his tail. It's his play bow.
- bow and then hop forward and backward.

When your dog is scared he might...
- whine.
- hold his tail between his legs.
- lower his head, ears, and tail.

When your dog is angry and wants to be left alone he might...
- stand with his tail and ears sticking straight up.
- growl.
- point his ears forward or turn them sideways.
- puff up the fur on his back.
- show his teeth and bark or growl.
- stare straight at what's annoying him.
- hold his tail in a downward curve.

When Do We Need To Visit the Veterinarian?

When you first bring your dog home, call your veterinarian and tell him or her you have a new dog. Set up an appointment for a visit. At your first visit, your doctor will check your dog's health and let you know when to come back for his shots and neutering. After that, you'll only have to go back once a year, unless he's sick or hurt.

Pay attention to your dog's health and behavior to know when he might be sick. When you notice that his behavior changes — he's coughing all the time, he's drinking water all the time, he's not excited to play—it may be time to visit the veterinarian.

Signs that your dog might be sick:

- Seems tired and doesn't want to play for more than one day
- Won't eat, or suddenly eating too much
- Coughing
- Diarrhea or constipation
- Drinks lots of water, or not enough water
- Coat is dull or has bald spots
- Panting a lot, even though he hasn't exercised
- Vomiting
- Drooling more than normal
- Gums are pale or swollen
- Extreme itching or scratching
- Swelling anywhere on body
- Lots of discharge in the eyes, nose, or ears
- Limping
- Eyes are puffy or red
- Very bad smell in ears or mouth

CHAPTER 4:
Your New Cat

If you've chosen to bring a cat to your home, you're not alone. Cats are favorite pets of thousands of people around the world, and they have been for many years. About 5,000 years ago, cats first started finding their way into people's homes where they helped families by hunting and killing pesky mice, rats, and snakes. They still have these hunting instincts, which you'll see when they "hunt" toy mice. But now most house cats are just as happy sleeping on your lap as they are hunting.

Not too long ago, there were only a few breeds of cats. Over the years some breeders made new breeds of cats. Cats from different breeds not only look different, but they can behave differently, too. Some breeds are more playful, some love to sit on a warm lap, and some like to meow all the time. But whichever kind of cat you choose, you're sure to love your new friend!

Cat Facts

- Cats belong to the same family of animals as tigers, lions, leopards, and panthers.

- Cats can run up to 48 kilometers (30 miles) per hour.

- Cats use their tails to help keep their balance.

- Cats twist their bodies in the air when they fall to land on their feet.

- Cats have special scent glands on their faces. When they rub their faces on furniture— or you—they leave their scent. It's their way of saying, "This is mine."

- Cats see differently than people. They can tell the difference between blue, green, and yellow, but don't seem to notice red. Cats see most colors in shades of gray. But cats can see movement much better than people.

- Cats have a third eyelid in the inner corner of their eyes.

- Cats have a special group of cells in the backs of their eyes. The tapetum lucidum reflects light inside a cat's eye to help it see in low light. The tapetum lucidum is also what makes a cat's eyes glow when a light shines on its eyes in the dark.

- Cats have rough tongues that help them keep their coats clean.

- Cats can move one ear in one direction, and the other ear in another direction.

- Cats can hear more sounds than people. Few cats are deaf, but more white cats with blue eyes or odd-colored eyes (each eye is a different color) are deaf.

- Cats use their whiskers to help sense things around them. From tip to tip, the whiskers on a cat's face show the smallest space a cat is comfortable walking through.

What Do I Need?

Before you bring your new cat home, you need to make sure your home is ready for her. That means everything from having a spot picked out for the food dish, to cat-proofing your home for her safety, to having all of the supplies needed to make her comfortable in her new home. (Look on page 63 for a list of things you'll need that you can copy and take with you when you shop.) On the next few pages you'll find the most important supplies you'll need for your new cat, and learn why you need them.

Food and Water

Obviously, you're going to need cat food, but there're many kinds of cat foods to choose from. There's dry food and wet food, food made especially for kittens or older cats, foods that have ingredients to help control hairball production in cats, and many more. You could spend an entire afternoon at the pet store staring at rows and rows of cat food. Make it easy on yourself and ask an expert, such as your veterinarian, for help in choosing the right food for your cat.

You'll also need a bowl for food and a bowl for water. Your cat's food and water bowls should be made of metal, ceramic, stainless steel, or glass. Plastic bowls aren't the best choice because they may get scratches where bacteria can grow and make your cat sick. The bowls should be stable so that they aren't easily tipped over. Keep the food and water bowls away from the litter box and in a place that your cat can easily get to, but that you or your family members won't trip over. A plastic placemat under the bowls will help keep the area clean and dry.

Most cats older than one year need to be fed twice a day, kittens need food more often. Check with your veterinarian to be sure about how often to feed your cat. Feed her at the same times every day. If she comes into your room before you wake up, meowing for food, don't get up and feed her. If you give in once, she'll know you'll give in again. Soon you'll be waking up when *she* wants you to wake up.

Many people leave a bowl full of dry cat food for their cats. This is sometimes called free feeding. If you do this, make sure you only use dry food and don't give your cat more food than she should get in one day (or she may gain too much weight).

If you decide to feed your cat a different kind of cat food, do it slowly. A complete change in food from one day to the next may give her an upset stomach, or she may simply refuse to eat. Mix in a little of the new food with the old food. After a couple of days mix in more of the new food so you have a mixture that is half old food and half new food. After a couple of days fill your cat's bowl with mostly new food and a little of the old food. A couple of days after that, your cat should be ready to make the switch to a bowl with just the new food.

If you feed your cat wet food, throw away any uneaten food that's been sitting out for more than half an hour. Change your cat's water at least twice a day, and make sure she always has plenty of water. Clean the bowls with soap and water a couple of times a week (don't use any bleaches or strong chemicals).

Although it's tempting to give your cat scraps from your plate, don't. Some foods may make your cat sick, and other foods may even kill her. So no matter how much she keeps nosing around your bowl of chocolate ice cream, don't give in! (In fact, chocolate can kill a cat!) Always only feed your cat food made especially for cats.

Litter Box

All cats need a litter box, but where should you put it? A litter box can be big and take up a lot of floor space, and you probably don't want to spend your day looking at a litter box. (Plus your cat may prefer some privacy!) So choose a place with plenty of room that's somewhat hidden—such as the laundry room, basement, or bathroom—and that

your cat can get in and out of easily. If you don't have a separate room where you can keep your cat's litter box, find a corner in your bedroom or living room and put a foldable screen in front of the box. A mat under the box to collect any loose litter that falls out of the box when your cat exits will help keep the area clean. You may also want to think about buying a covered litter box. They cost more, but will keep things from falling into the box. Whatever spot you choose, keep the litter box there. Moving the box to a different room may confuse your cat, and she may make a mistake.

A lot of people worry about the smell of a cat's litter box. But if you keep the box clean, this shouldn't be a problem. Plus, if you don't keep the box clean, your cat may decide to find a cleaner spot to use, like the rug in a corner of your bedroom. Once a cat starts using your floor or rug as a litter box, it will be very hard to get her to stop. So keep her box clean and easy to reach. Use a slotted spoon or shovel to scoop out any solids from the box. You should do this at least once a day. Every couple of weeks, throw away everything inside of the litter box. Clean it with soap and water, dry it, put down a litter liner, and then fill the box with fresh litter. You don't have to use a litter liner, but it can make clean-up time quicker and easier for you.

Most cats know how to use a litter box. But if you have a very young kitten, or decide to let a stray into your home, she may need some help. For the first few days, keep the cat in a small room with the litter box in plain view. Place the cat in the box every time after she eats until she gets used to going on her own. Once she starts using the litter box, you can put the box in its permanent place. You may want to lead her to the box after she eats for the first few days after you've put the box in its permanent spot to make sure she knows where it is.

Scratching Post

A cat doesn't scratch your favorite chair because she wants to destroy it; she scratches it because she *has* to scratch. Scratching is the way cats get rid of the worn outer layers of their claws. So if you want to keep your furniture, curtains, and those brand-new jeans you left hanging off your bed from being shredded, give her something she can scratch—a scratching post.

Your cat will probably need some help getting the hang of using a new scratching post, especially if she's never used one before. Guide her front paws down the post, like she does when scratching. Rubbing some catnip on the post may be a way to get her to pay attention to the post. Whenever you catch her trying to scratch something else, say "No!" and immediately take her to the post and guide her paws down the post.

Some people choose to have their cats declawed. Declawing is an operation that removes the claws of your cat's front paws. If your cat uses her scratching post, and only scratches the furniture or curtains from time to time, you may not want to declaw her. (And remember, it may take some time for her to get used to using the scratching post.) Without her front claws, she is pretty much defenseless. This is especially important to know if you plan to let her spend time outdoors.

Catnip is a strong-smelling (to cats, anyway) herb that most cats go crazy over. People often rub catnip on toys or other things they want their cats to use. For a treat, fill the tip of an old sock with catnip. Tie off the sock and let your cat enjoy her new "toy."

Grooming Tools

Cats do a very good job of keeping themselves clean, but sometimes they need a little help. Plus, combing and brushing your cat is a great way to relax and bond with her—and it helps prevent hairballs from forming. Make sure the comb and brush you buy is right for your cat; longhaired cats need different ones than shorthaired cats. Longhaired cats also need more brushing than shorthaired cats.

Longhaired cats may need combing and brushing several times a day.

Start by brushing the hair on her back, from head to tail. Then gently comb the fur between her back legs and front legs. If you find a knot, use your fingers to untangle it. Then comb the hair on her stomach. Be extra gentle around her stomach. This area is very sensitive for cats and they don't like being touched there too much. Finally comb upward behind her ears and under her chin.

Shorthaired cats need only a quick brushing a couple of times a week. Gently brush your cat all over, from head to tail.

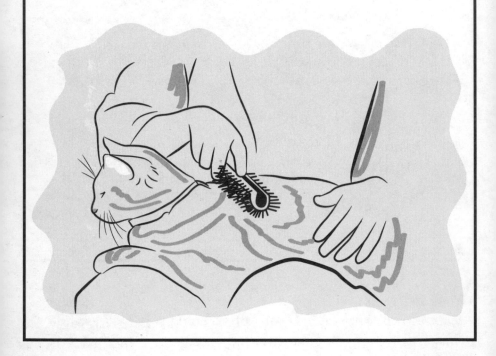

Even if your cat is an indoor cat, chances are she'll have fleas at some point in her life. A couple of times a month use a fine-toothed flea comb to check her for fleas. Fleas look like dark sesame seeds (and they'll jump or move very quickly) and their droppings look like black pepper. If she's got fleas, it's time for a flea bath. A professional groomer can bathe her, or you can do it yourself. Bathe her in lukewarm water with flea shampoo made especially for cats. Make sure you buy the right shampoo for her age and follow the instructions on the label carefully. Then check with your veterinarian to find out if your cat should be on a flea treatment.

Most cats don't need regular baths. They keep themselves pretty clean and too much bathing can be bad for their skin or coat. But there may be times when she'll need one, so it's a good idea to bathe her once every two or three months so when she does need a bath it's less stressful for her.

First, have everything ready before you get your cat. Use the bathtub or bathroom sink so you can close the door to the bathroom and give your cat a quiet room for bathing. You'll also need cat shampoo, a large cup (for pouring water), and a towel.
Choose a time for bathing when your cat is relaxed (but not asleep). Pet her and talk calmly to her as you take her to the bathroom. Close the door and gently put her inside the tub or sink.

Slowly start to pour lukewarm water over your cat, starting with her rear, then back, and finally face. Squeeze a little shampoo onto her back and massage it into her fur. Then rinse her off with more water.

Take her out of the tub and wrap her in the towel. Gently press the towel to her fur to squeeze out the water. Don't use a hair dryer—the noise and heat may upset your cat and make bath time a scary time for her.

Make sure to keep her warm until she's completely dry. Put her down in a sunny spot with the towel. Don't be upset if she doesn't want to be around you at first. Walk away and let her warm up in peace.

Another grooming tool you'll need is a cat nail clipper. If done correctly clipping your cat's nails isn't painful, but she probably won't like it. For your first nail-clipping session, it's a good idea to have your veterinarian show you how to do it. At home, you may want to work with an adult helper until you and your cat are comfortable with the procedure. Choose a time when your cat is calm, not when she's ready to play. Speaking calmly to her while you're trimming her claws will help keep her calm.

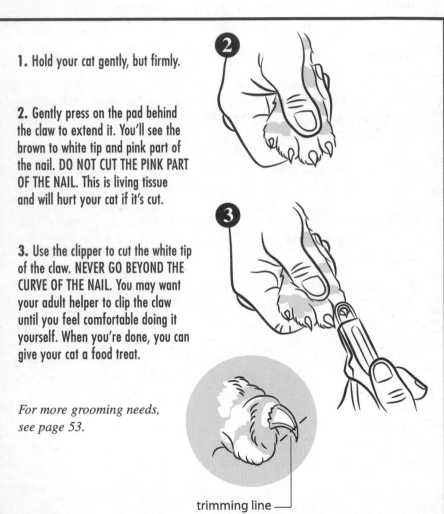

1. Hold your cat gently, but firmly.

2. Gently press on the pad behind the claw to extend it. You'll see the brown to white tip and pink part of the nail. DO NOT CUT THE PINK PART OF THE NAIL. This is living tissue and will hurt your cat if it's cut.

3. Use the clipper to cut the white tip of the claw. NEVER GO BEYOND THE CURVE OF THE NAIL. You may want your adult helper to clip the claw until you feel comfortable doing it yourself. When you're done, you can give your cat a food treat.

For more grooming needs,
see page 53.

trimming line

Collar and Identification Tag

Even if you plan to never let your cat outdoors, that doesn't mean she'll have the same plans. Cats like to explore, and a door to the backyard you forgot to close is too tempting for her to ignore! And she can get pretty far if you don't notice right away that she's escaped. So make sure your cat has a collar and identification tag ready for her the day you bring her home.

Cat collars come in all kinds of colors. The important thing is that the collar is tight enough on her so that she can't slip it off her head, but not too tight to make her uncomfortable.

Her identification tag should have your name, telephone number, and address on it. If you've already chosen a name for her, you can add that to the tag, too. When you visit the veterinarian, find out about having your cat tattooed or injected with a microchip for a more permanent kind of identification.

Cat Carrier

Any time you travel with your cat, you need to put her in a cat carrier. If you're picking up a small kitten from a shelter, you can use an inexpensive cardboard carrier. By the time you take her to her first visit to the veterinarian, however, you should have a sturdier plastic carrier. Buy one that will fit her as she grows older.

Keeping the carrier out where she can see it and nap inside whenever she wants to will help her feel comfortable with it. If the only time she sees the carrier is when she has to go to the veterinarian, she'll know it's bad news and will hide from you whenever you bring it out. You can put a towel or blanket inside and a few small toys so she'll see the carrier as a cozy place to rest.

Bed

Cats have no problem finding a spot to sleep—and they average an amazing 16 hours of sleep every day! But unless you want her shedding on the couch, the chair, and your bed, it's a good idea to give

her a place that's just hers. You can buy a cat bed, or use things you have at home to make one. A wicker basket or cardboard box (with a small entrance cut into it) large enough to fit your cat makes a good bed. Put a clean towel or blanket inside to make her bed soft. Place the bed by a sunny window and she'll be more tempted to use it.

Toys

Part of keeping your cat happy is making sure she has fun. They don't have to be expensive, but toys are a must for every cat. The best toys are the kinds that move—small balls she can chase, or toys that hang from strings or rods that you drag for her to run after. Even something

as simple as jumping into and onto a paper bag, or pouncing on the light from a flashlight you shine across the floor will entertain her for a long time.

Play with your cat for at least 15 minutes twice a day. But don't use your hands or feet as "toys." Cats scratch and bite their toys. Once you start using your hands as her toy, she may bite you—or a visitor—when she's feeling playful.

Cat-Proofing Your Home

Cats, especially kittens, are very curious. They love to swat and climb things that hang, and drag and push over things that stick out. They'll jump up to places that seem much too high for a cat to reach, and hang out in spots that look much too small to fit a cat. They'll even wiggle into cupboards and closets you know had closed doors. This is part of what makes cats fun and cute. But this can make your home a dangerous place for your cat. You'll need to give your home a safety inspection a day before your new cat comes to live with you to make sure she's as safe as possible.

Keep electrical cords, telephone cords, and the cords to your window blinds tucked away or tied up and out of reach. Put away any string (including dental floss). Anything breakable that's on a shelf or table should be put somewhere safer. Keep the toilet seat down all the time so your cat doesn't accidentally fall in (and maybe drown). Always keep the door to the washing machine and dryer closed. Get used to keeping your closet door closed or she's bound to walk in there and make a mess. Keep windows closed, or screens in place, if you don't want your cat escaping.

Some things can be very dangerous to your cat, making her sick or even poisoning her. Make sure all pesticides (including roach and ant traps) and household cleaners are kept in cabinets where she can't get into. Keep all medicines where she can't reach them. Even some plants can be dangerous to cats. This list shows some of the more common plants that should be kept out of homes with cats. If you're not sure about a plant, check with your veterinarian to make sure it's is safe for your cat.

Dangerous Plants

Aloe vera	Hemlock	Oleander
Asparagus fern	Larkspur	Philodendron
Azalea	Laurel	Poinsettia
Bittersweet	Lily of the valley	Spider plant
Caladium	Mistletoe	Wisteria
English ivy		

The Right Way To Pick Up Your Cat

You could hurt your cat if you don't know the right way to pick her up. When you want to pick up your cat, talk calmly to her and walk in front of her. Don't sneak up behind her and grab her. This will scare her and she may react by scratching you, or else she might learn to be afraid of you. Pet her for a moment and then walk to her side so both of you are facing the same direction. Then put one hand under her back legs, and the other hand under her chest.

If your cat doesn't like being picked up, work with her. Start by picking her up, then putting her right back down. Do this several times a day, always talking calmly to her and telling her what a good girl she's being. After a few days, start picking her up and holding her a little longer each time. It may take a few weeks, but she'll eventually get used to having you hold her.

The Well-Groomed Cat

Cats are well known for being very clean animals. And you help her stay healthy and look her best with brushings and occasional baths (see page 47). But when it comes to her eyes, ears, and teeth, she needs a little more help from you.

Eyes

Check her eyes every day for any discharge. Use a tissue or a wet cotton ball to gently wipe around her eyes especially in the corners. If you notice that her eyes are glazed, puffy, red, or have a lot of discharge, you should call your veterinarian. (For more signs that you may need to call the veterinarian, see page 58.)

Ears

Next check your cat's ears. Look for dirt, waxy buildup, and grainy, dry discharge (this could mean she has ear mites). Put a drop of ear-cleaning solution (made for cats) on a cotton ball and wipe the inside of her ears. Then put a drop of the solution on a cotton swab and clean her ear canals. Because you need to be very careful not to go too deep into her canals, you may need to ask your veterinarian show you how to do it the first time. If you find ear mites, you should call your veterinarian. (For more signs that you may need to call the veterinarian, see page 58.)

Teeth

Finally, brush your cat's teeth. If you ignore her teeth she may end up with tooth decay. Use a cotton swab to rub across her teeth. Pay special attention to the back teeth. You can also use a toothbrush and toothpaste made especially for cats. If you notice that her gums are pale or swollen or her breath smells especially bad, you should call your veterinarian. (For more signs that you may need to call the veterinarian, see page 58.)

Training Your Cat

Cats are well known for doing their own thing, but they can be trained if you're consistent and persistent. That means if she's not allowed on the countertops when there's food there, then she's NEVER allowed on the countertops. Letting her jump onto the countertops when there's no food, but not letting her when there is food is just too confusing for her. And don't give up trying to train her even if she doesn't seem to be listening. It takes lots and lots of patience to train a cat.

Training sessions should only last a few minutes and you should chose times to train when she is awake, calm, and not distracted watching the birds outside your window. Don't yell at her while training; you can say "No!" firmly without yelling. And NEVER hit your cat. This just makes her afraid of you.

With some patience, you can teach your cat to come to you when you call her. This is especially important if she's an outdoor cat. Using a

food treat she loves, show it to her, take a step back, call her name, and say "Come." When she comes, let her have the treat. As you continue to train, take more and more steps back. When she is coming to you every time you call her, stop giving her the treat every time. Instead, be ready to play a quick game with her or give her a quick cuddle.

When Your Cat Misbehaves

- Say "No!" sharply; then show her what she should be doing (like using her scratching post), or give her a toy so she can play

- Give her a quick squirt from a water bottle

- Shake an emptied soda can you've filled with several pennies

Rewarding Your Cat

- Cuddle her, or spend some time petting her

- Bring out the toys and play with her

- Give her a food treat

You can't always be there to correct your cat's behavior. But there are some things you can do to keep her from misbehaving when you're not around. If she's jumping onto counters, tables, or furniture that are off-limits to her, cover the surface with double-sided tape. Most cats don't like anything sticky on their paws. You can also fill several emptied soda cans with a few pennies each (tape over the opening) and then place them along the edge of the countertops or tables. The loud, scary noise these cans make when she jumps up there will keep her away.

What's My Cat Trying To Tell Me?

Your cat may not be able to talk, but with a purr, a meow, and a slow rub against you legs, she can definitely communicate with you. As you get to know your cat, you'll know by how she behaves if she's happy, scared, or wants to be left alone. And when your cat wants to be alone, leave her alone. If you try to pick her up now, she might scratch you as she tries to defend herself (even if you were only trying to calm her down). It's not her fault—she tried to warn you—so you can't let yourself get angry with her. If she's scared or angry, give her time to calm down.

When your cat is happy and relaxed she might...
- purr or meow.
- walk up to you with her tail raised straight up, or with her tail relaxed.
- lay on her stomach with her eyes half closed.
- sit on your lap and lick your hands and arms.
- press with her paws on your stomach or legs.

When your cat wants to play she might...
- roll over on her side in front of you.
- run up to you, tap you lightly with a paw, and run away.
- dart around you as you walk.

When your cat is scared she might...
- curve her back.
- puff out her fur.
- turn sideways and hop forward.
- hiss or growl.
- hide under a bed or couch, or climb to a spot that's up high.
- flatten her whiskers against her face.

When your cat is angry and wants to be left alone she might...
- stare straight at what's annoying her.
- growl.
- crouch low on the ground.
- make her pupils very large, or make her pupils into wide slits.
- flatten her ears back against her head.
- hold her tail in a downward curve.
- push her whiskers forward.

When Do We Need To Visit the Veterinarian?

When you first bring your cat home, call your veterinarian and tell him or her you have a new cat. Set up an appointment for a visit. At your first visit, your doctor will check your cat's health and let you know when to come back for her vaccinations and neutering. After that, you'll only have to go back once a year, unless she's sick or hurt.

Since you'll be spending the most time with your cat, you'll get to know her behavior pretty well. When you notice that her behavior changes—she's not eating, she's drinking water all the time, she's scratching more —it may be time to visit the veterinarian.

Signs that your cat might be sick:

- Vomiting
- Drooling
- Extreme itching or scratching
- Coughing or sneezing
- Seems tired all the time
- Bumps on the inside of the thighs
- Swelling anywhere on body
- Lots of wax or dark discharge in ears
- Won't eat, or suddenly eating too much
- Gums and tongue are pale or dark red
- Diarrhea or constipation
- Drinking lots of water
- Coat is dull or has bald spots
- Very bad breath
- Eyes are red, puffy, dull, or glazed

CHAPTER 5:
Digital Pets

Maybe soccer practice and homework leave you with little free time after school and on the weekends. Maybe you always have to be the first of your friends to get the latest, greatest digital gadget. Maybe just being in the same room with a dog or a cat makes you sneeze uncontrollably. Maybe you're just not sure you're ready for the real thing. Whatever the reason, you've chosen a digital pet as a new best friend. And they're becoming so popular, some people think that digital pets will outnumber the real thing one day!

There're several kinds of digital pets, sometimes called electronic pets or virtual pets. They can cost anywhere from a few dollars to hundreds—even thousands—of dollars. They're basically toys, but people love them as if they were a living, breathing animal.

Digital pets need attention, just like the real thing. But unlike the real thing, you can turn off your digital pet if things get too crazy. And you don't have to worry that your digital pet might have an accident on your bed, or wake you up in the middle of the night because it wants to play.

Most digital pets have sensors that let them react to your voice and to your commands. If the pet hears a command it recognizes, such as "walk," it reacts by following the command. Most commands are simple and use only a few words. Some pets will even sing if you clap your hands in a certain pattern. And if you get several of these pets together, they can all sing together and interact with one another!

With most of the popular digital pets, it's important to remember a few important things if you want your pet to follow commands:

- Say your pet's name quickly.
- Always say your pet's name before giving it a command.
- After you say your pet's name, wait until it responds. Its eyes, cheeks, or a small bulb on the top if its head flashes to show you it recognized its name.
- Then give the command in the same quick voice you used to say its name.

Virtual pets also have their own unique personalities and moods. Just like real pets, virtual pets are happy if you pay attention to them, annoyed if you give them too many commands, and sulky if you ignore them. You can usually tell its mood by the noises it makes. It might chirp in a way that sounds like laughter when it's happy. Or it might moan and groan to show you it's annoyed by all of your commands. And don't forget to praise it when its done a good job or it might get so upset that it refuses to follow any more of your commands!

Even digital pets need some grooming from time to time. Keep it clean by wiping it with a damp cloth about once a week. Keeping your digital pet "healthy" includes making sure its batteries are fresh. Don't leave old batteries inside of your pet. They might leak and ruin your pet. When the batteries need to be changed, follow the instructions that came with your pet.

The more expensive your electronic pet is, the more it's able to do. Some of these pets can respond to 50 commands or more (the less expensive ones respond to about 10 commands). The pricier pets have computers in them that act like a brain. They can even learn like real dogs and cats-if you say "No!" they remember the next time and don't misbehave. And if you praise them, they know they've done something good.

You can also find virtual pets on the Internet. Some sites let you create a pet with its own likes and dislikes. And the kind of pet you choose can be anything from a monkey, to a unicorn, to an alien. These sites are free and you can play games, solve puzzles, and go on quests with your pet. You keep your virtual pet happy by giving it food and toys it likes.

So even though they can't fall asleep on your lap or lick your face hello, a digital pet can be just as loveable and fun as a real dog or a cat.

FORMS TO COPY

To use the forms on the following pages, cut along the dotted lines.
Then make photocopies of the pages you need.
Keep the Pet File sheet somewhere you can find it quickly
so you can update it after every visit to the veterinarian.

Dog Supply List

Must Buy

- ☐ Food bowl
- ☐ Water bowl
- ☐ Plastic mat
- ☐ Food
- ☐ Dog treats
- ☐ Crate
- ☐ Brush
- ☐ Comb
- ☐ Flea comb
- ☐ Dog nail clipper
- ☐ Leash
- ☐ Collar
- ☐ Identification tag
- ☐ Toys

Maybe Buy

- ☐ Dog bed
- ☐ Dog shampoo
- ☐ Dog toothbrush
- ☐ Dog toothpaste
- ☐ Car barrier or dog harness
- ☐ Car window screen